MASS FOR FOUR VOICES

BY

WILLIAM BYRD

EDITED AND ARRANGED FOR MODERN USE BY

HENRY WASHINGTON

———————

Duration of performance 30 minutes

———————

CHESTER MUSIC
part of **WiseMusic**Group

EXCLUSIVELY DISTRIBUTED BY

HAL•LEONARD®

PREFACE

THIS new transcription of Byrd's Masses for three, four and five voices respectively has been prepared mainly to meet the demand for a practical choir edition. Although these masterpieces of Tudor polyphony have long been familiar through earlier transcriptions by Rimbault, Rockstro, Barclay Squire, Terry and Fellowes a few textual uncertainties have persisted. I have therefore used the occasion to make a definitive score by reference to the set of original part-books in the British Museum. Thus for the first time in a separate publication of these works any editorial suggestions are readily distinguishable from the original text. Byrd's own accidentals are printed in the normal position, i.e. to the left of the note affected while other accidentals, added for whatever reason, appear in small type above the note. A system of regular barring has been applied having regard to the fact that the training and equipment of the present-day choral singer bear little relation to those of his sixteenth-century counterpart. Experience has shown that any visual advantage to the rhythmic flow derived from irregular barring is diminished in practice by difficulties of counting and place-finding.

The music text is here set out unencumbered with arbitrary marks of expression. In this way the director is free to insert such guides to performance as he thinks expedient, and singers are spared the confusion induced by his insistence on, say, a *pianissimo* reading when the edited score demands a contrary effect. A suggested scheme of interpretation is incorporated in the *reductio partiturae*. The sign *p̌* , a short vertical stroke placed above or below a note, is freely used in this edition with the twofold object of defending verbal rhythm against the accentual power associated with the modern bar-line, and of defining the true agogic rhythm where an original long note has been replaced by two tied notes of shorter duration. Sixteenth-century note-values have been halved to accord with later acceptance of the crotchet as the normal unit of time. The slur is used solely to denote a ligature.

Three misprints are to be found in the original notation of the present Mass for Four Voices. In each of the first two the final Bassus note of a section is printed a third too low. (p. 5, bar 31 and p.19, bar 53). The third misprint occurs in the Sanctus (p. 30, bar 3) where the original Altus part falls an augmented fourth on the second half of the first beat. *Tudor Church Music* and Fellowes substitute a third above this note, perhaps on the analogy of the two previous faults, but as this solution does not bear scrutiny I have regarded the misprint as of one degree too high, a type of error to be found in the original of the Mass for Three Voices. The resulting figure is a melodic cliché of the Tudor composer, although it found little favour with the Roman school. Byrd employs it often in the three and four-part Masses either for consonant melody or, as in the present case, for disjunct resolution of a suspension. A curious misprint of two adjacent notes in the Fellowes edition is noted on p.22.

I have used discretion in underlaying the verbal text. Byrd's melodic genius often defies the strict application of such rules for word-placing as have come down to us from the theorists of his day. Moreover, the English peculiarities in this matter referred to by the editors of *T.C.M.* are not always valid in the case of Byrd's Mass music, to go no further than that. In particular reference to the Mass for Four Voices it should be noted that the *Kyrie eleison* melodies imply elision of the final E in the word *Kyrie*. Where this occurs the silent E is printed in italics.

HENRY WASHINGTON

THE ORATORY,
    LONDON,
        March, 1959

MASS FOR FOUR VOICES

KYRIE

WILLIAM BYRD
Edited by
HENRY WASHINGTON

4

GLORIA

CREDO

* Fellowes reads FG.

SANCTUS

BENEDICTUS

AGNUS DEI

38

8803